YOU'RE A STAR!

summersdale

YOU'RE A STAR

Image on p.1 © Mascha Tace/Shutterstock.com
Star icon on pp.6, 13, 18, 36, 43, 48, 66, 73, 78, 96, 193, 108, 126, 133, 138 and 156 © Alex Kednert/Shutterstock.com

Research by Giada Nizzoli

Summersdale Publishers Ltd
46 West Street
Chichester
West Sussex
PO19 1RP
UK

www.summersdale.com

Printed and bound in the Czech Republic

ISBN: 978-1-78685-202-1

Substantial discounts on bulk quantities of Summersdale books are available to corporations, professional associations and other organisations. For details contact general enquiries: telephone: +44 (0) 1243 771107 or email: enquiries@summersdale.com.

To...........................

From.......................

YOU ARE
ONE OF A KIND.

FOLLOW YOUR INNER MOONLIGHT;

DON'T HIDE THE MADNESS.

Allen Ginsberg

Keep your eyes on the stars, and your feet on the ground.

Theodore Roosevelt

You are braver than you believe,
stronger than you seem,
and smarter than you think.

A. A. Milne

BE YOURSELF. THE
WORLD WORSHIPS
THE ORIGINAL.

Ingrid Bergman

Nothing can stop you.

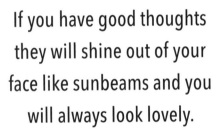

If you have good thoughts
they will shine out of your
face like sunbeams and you
will always look lovely.

Roald Dahl

LET US LEARN TO SHOW OUR
FRIENDSHIP FOR A MAN WHEN HE IS
ALIVE AND NOT AFTER HE IS DEAD.

F. Scott Fitzgerald

RIDE THE ENERGY
OF YOUR OWN
UNIQUE SPIRIT.

Gabrielle Roth

Find ecstasy in life; the mere sense of living is joy enough.

Emily Dickinson

You make everything sparkle!

**YOUR ATTITUDE IS LIKE
A BOX OF CRAYONS THAT
COLOUR YOUR WORLD.**

Allen Klein

Good friends help you find important things when you have lost them… your smile, your hope, and your courage.

Doe Zantamata

Never dull your shine for somebody else.

Tyra Banks

**Shoot for the moon.
Even if you fail
you'll land
among the stars.**

Les Brown

START YOUR DAY WITH A SMILE.

TALK TO YOURSELF LIKE YOU
WOULD TO SOMEONE YOU LOVE.

Brené Brown

LIGHT TOMORROW
WITH TODAY.

Elizabeth Barrett Browning

Dwell on the beauty of life.
Watch the stars, and see
yourself running with them.

Marcus Aurelius

You've got
the power.

To love yourself right now,
just as you are, is to give
yourself heaven.

Alan Cohen

Try to be a rainbow
in someone's cloud.

Maya Angelou

IF YOU THINK YOU CAN DO IT, YOU CAN.

John Burroughs

I would rather walk
with a friend in the dark
than walk alone in the light.

Helen Keller

YOU ARE MY SUPERHERO!

WHY NOT JUST LIVE IN THE MOMENT, ESPECIALLY IF IT HAS A GOOD BEAT?

Goldie Hawn

To live with a feeling of fulfilment is the greatest blessings for any human being.

Paramahamsa Nithyananda

MAY YOU LIVE ALL THE DAYS OF YOUR LIFE.

Jonathan Swift

Believe in yourself.
Pick a path that you,
deep down in your soul,
won't be ashamed of.

Hiromu Arakawa

FOLLOW YOUR
DREAMS.

ALWAYS BE A FIRST-RATE
VERSION OF YOURSELF AND
NOT A SECOND-RATE VERSION
OF SOMEONE ELSE.

Judy Garland

Do not doubt the goodness in you.

Dodinsky

The person who can bring
the spirit of laughter into
a room is indeed blessed.

Bennett Cerf

THE DREAMERS
ARE THE SAVIOURS
OF THE WORLD.

James Allen

Be the spice in your own life.

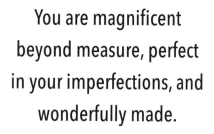

You are magnificent
beyond measure, perfect
in your imperfections, and
wonderfully made.

Abiola Abrams

**WHEREVER YOU ARE
— BE ALL THERE.**

Jim Elliot

WHY FIT IN
WHEN YOU WERE
BORN TO STAND OUT?

Dr Seuss

Let your dreams outgrow the shoes of your expectations.

Ryunosuke Satoro

There's no one
quite like you.

UNFOLD YOUR OWN MYTH.

Rumi

Those who bring sunshine
into the lives of others cannot
keep it from themselves.

J. M. Barrie

The greatest
healing therapy is
friendship and love.

Hubert Humphrey

Don't let what you cannot do interfere with what you can do.

John R. Wooden

YOU'RE THE
ICING ON MY
CAKE.

WHO LOOKS OUTSIDE, DREAMS;
WHO LOOKS INSIDE, AWAKES.

Carl Jung

**YOUR BIG OPPORTUNITY
MAY BE RIGHT
WHERE YOU ARE NOW.**

Napoleon Hill

Feeling gratitude and not
expressing it is like wrapping
a present and not giving it.

William Arthur Ward

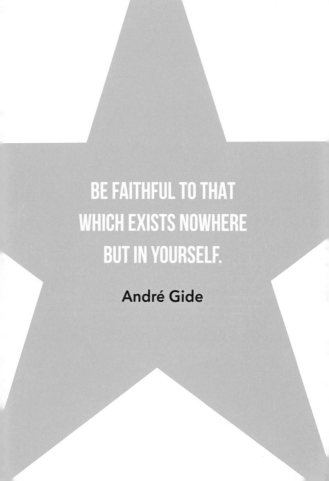

BE FAITHFUL TO THAT
WHICH EXISTS NOWHERE
BUT IN YOURSELF.

André Gide

I'm lucky I met someone like you.

Don't waste your energy
trying to change opinions…
do your thing, and don't
care if they like it.

Tina Fey

Be happy. It's one
way of being wise.

Colette

NOTHING CAN DIM
THE LIGHT WHICH
SHINES FROM WITHIN.

Maya Angelou

Trust yourself.
You know more than
you think you do.

Benjamin Spock

LIFE'S AN ADVENTURE: LIVE IT!

IN MY MOMENTS OF DOUBT
I'VE TOLD MYSELF FIRMLY:
IF NOT ME, WHO?
IF NOT NOW, WHEN?

Emma Watson

No one can make you feel
inferior without your consent.

Eleanor Roosevelt

YOU ARE VERY POWERFUL,
PROVIDED YOU KNOW HOW
POWERFUL YOU ARE.

Yogi Bhajan

The reward for conformity is
that everyone likes you
except yourself.

Rita Mae Brown

YOU ARE THE HERO OF YOUR STORY.

YOU CAN, YOU SHOULD,
AND IF YOU'RE BRAVE ENOUGH
TO START, YOU WILL.

Stephen King

A day without laughter is a day wasted.

Nicolas Chamfort

With confidence, you have won
even before you have started.

Marcus Garvey

DOUBT WHOM YOU WILL, BUT NEVER YOURSELF.

Christian Nestell Bovee

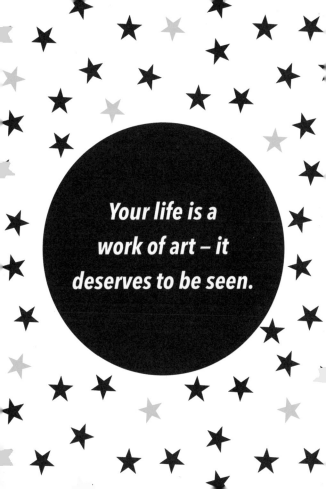

Your life is a work of art – it deserves to be seen.

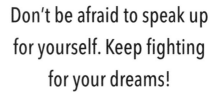

Don't be afraid to speak up
for yourself. Keep fighting
for your dreams!

Gabby Douglas

IT IS IMPORTANT IN LIFE
NOT TO BE STRONG, BUT
TO FEEL STRONG.

Jon Krakauer

NEVER CONSIDER THE POSSIBILITY OF FAILURE; AS LONG AS YOU PERSIST, YOU WILL BE SUCCESSFUL.

Brian Tracy

Opportunity dances with those who are already on the dance floor.

H. Jackson Brown

You can do it!

ONE JOY SCATTERS
A HUNDRED GRIEFS.

Chinese proverb

Good friends are like stars;
you don't always see them
but you know they're there.

Anonymous

Life shrinks or expands in proportion to one's courage.

Anaïs Nin

Self-care is never
a selfish act.

Parker J. Palmer

SEIZE THAT OPPORTUNITY.

**DO NOT FORGET YOUR DUTY
TO LOVE YOURSELF.**

Søren Kierkegaard

IT ALWAYS SEEMS
IMPOSSIBLE
UNTIL IT'S DONE.

Anonymous

A strong, positive self-image
is the best possible
preparation for success.

Joyce Brothers

BE UNAPOLOGETICALLY YOU.

Steve Maraboli

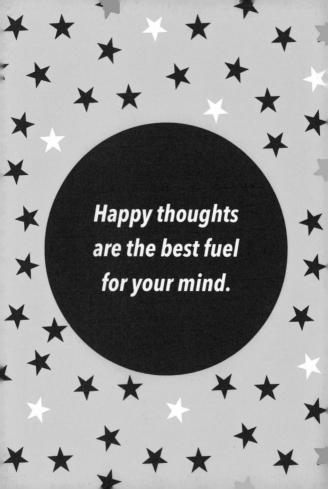

Happy thoughts are the best fuel for your mind.

It doesn't matter where
you are coming from.
All that matters is
where you are going.

Brian Tracy

The first step
is you have to
say that you can.

Will Smith

AIM HIGH!
THE FUTURE YOU
SEE, IS THE PERSON
YOU WILL BE.

Jim Cathcart

Sometimes people
are beautiful. Not in looks.
Not in what they say.
Just in what they are.

Markus Zusak

LIVE YOUR
DREAMS.

PLUNGE BOLDLY INTO THE THICK OF LIFE, AND SEIZE IT WHERE YOU WILL.

Johann Wolfgang von Goethe

Keep smiling, because life
is beautiful and there's
so much to smile about.

Marilyn Monroe

**LOVE CASTS OUT
FEAR, AND GRATITUDE
CAN CONQUER PRIDE.**

Louisa May Alcott

Always be yourself…
do not go out and look for
a successful personality
and try to duplicate it.

Bruce Lee

BELIEVE YOU CAN AND YOU WILL.

**AN UNSHARED HAPPINESS
IS NOT HAPPINESS.**

Boris Pasternak

I'd rather aim
high and miss, than
aim low and hit.

Les Brown

It is not wrong to be different. Sometimes it is hard, but it is not wrong.

Elizabeth Moon

FRIENDSHIP, LIKE PHOSPHORUS, SHINES BRIGHTEST WHEN ALL AROUND IS DARK.

Anonymous

Take time to do what makes your soul happy.

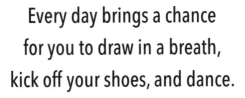

Every day brings a chance
for you to draw in a breath,
kick off your shoes, and dance.

Oprah Winfrey

HAVE PATIENCE WITH ALL THINGS,
BUT FIRST OF ALL WITH YOURSELF.

Francis de Sales

SOME PEOPLE
GO TO PRIESTS;
OTHERS TO POETRY;
I TO MY FRIENDS.

Virginia Woolf

**Don't be a blueprint.
Be an original.**

Roy Acuff

If you don't believe in magic, you will never find it.

PUT YOUR FUTURE IN
GOOD HANDS — YOUR OWN.

Anonymous

A friend is someone
whose face you can
see in the dark.

Frances O'Roark Dowell

Treasure the
magnificent being
that you are.

Wayne W. Dyer

**A smile is
a curve that sets
everything straight.**

Phyllis Diller

YOUR PERSONALITY LIGHTS UP THE WHOLE ROOM.

**YOUR ASPIRATIONS
ARE YOUR POSSIBILITIES.**

Samuel Johnson

ALWAYS ACT LIKE YOU'RE WEARING AN INVISIBLE CROWN.

Anonymous

For friendship makes prosperity more shining and lessens adversity by dividing and sharing it.

Cicero

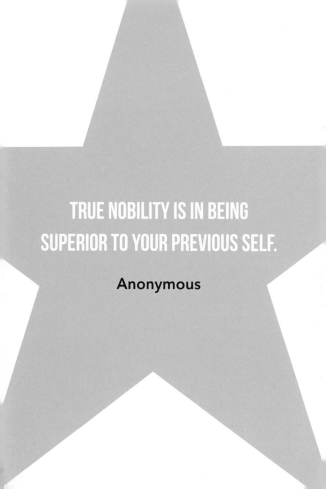

TRUE NOBILITY IS IN BEING
SUPERIOR TO YOUR PREVIOUS SELF.

Anonymous

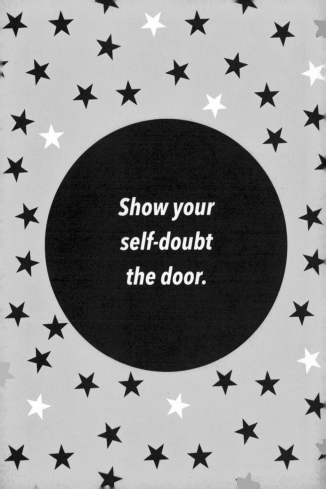

*Show your
self-doubt
the door.*

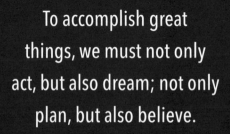

To accomplish great
things, we must not only
act, but also dream; not only
plan, but also believe.

Anatole France

A good laugh is
sunshine in the house.

William Makepeace
Thackeray

DARE TO BE DIFFERENT AND TO SET YOUR OWN PATTERN — LIVE YOUR OWN LIFE AND FOLLOW YOUR OWN STAR.

Wilfred Peterson

Don't let them tame you.

Isadora Duncan

I BELIEVE
IN YOU.

YOUR CHANCES OF SUCCESS IN ANY UNDERTAKING CAN ALWAYS BE MEASURED BY YOUR BELIEF IN YOURSELF.

Robert Collier

When you're true to who you
are, amazing things happen.

Deborah Norville

**HUMAN POTENTIAL IS
THE ONLY LIMITLESS RESOURCE
WE HAVE IN THIS WORLD.**

Carly Fiorina

Don't live down to
expectations. Go out there and
do something remarkable.

Wendy Wasserstein

YOU ROCK!

**LAUGHTER IS A
SUNBEAM OF THE SOUL.**

Thomas Mann

If you have nothing in life but a good friend, you are rich.

Michelle Kwan

If you obey all the rules
you miss all the fun.

Katharine Hepburn

HE WHO IS NOT
EVERYDAY CONQUERING
SOME FEAR HAS
NOT LEARNED THE
SECRET OF LIFE.

Ralph Waldo Emerson

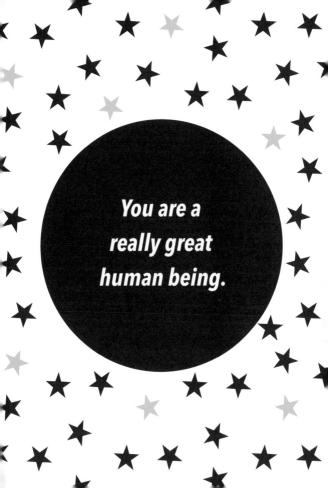

*You are a
really great
human being.*

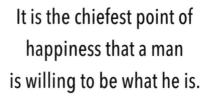

It is the chiefest point of
happiness that a man
is willing to be what he is.

Erasmus

IF YOU THINK YOU ARE TOO SMALL
TO MAKE A DIFFERENCE,
TRY SLEEPING WITH A MOSQUITO.

Dalai Lama

FOR A FRIEND WITH AN UNDERSTANDING HEART IS WORTH NO LESS THAN A BROTHER.

Homer

In order to be
irreplaceable one
must always
be different.

Coco Chanel

Write your own destiny.

THOSE WHO MATTER
DON'T MIND,
AND THOSE WHO MIND
DON'T MATTER.

Bernard Baruch

What progress, you ask, have I made? I have begun to be a friend to myself.

Hecato

Your spirit is
the true shield.

Morihei Ueshiba

Be not afraid of going slowly; be afraid only of standing still.

Chinese proverb

YOU ARE CAPABLE OF AMAZING THINGS.

IT IS OFTEN IN THE
DARKEST SKIES THAT WE SEE
THE BRIGHTEST STARS.

Richard Paul Evans

A GOOD COMPANION SHORTENS THE LONGEST ROAD.

Turkish proverb

Be brave enough to
live creatively... what you
discover will be wonderful.
What you discover
will be yourself.

Alan Alda

LIFE IS A PURE FLAME,
AND WE LIVE BY AN
INVISIBLE SUN WITHIN US.

Thomas Browne

Thank you for being in my life.

Wherever you go, no matter
what the weather, always
bring your own sunshine.

Anthony J. D'Angelo

Those who wish to sing
always find a song.

Swedish proverb

IT TAKES COURAGE TO GROW UP AND BECOME WHO YOU REALLY ARE.

E. E. Cummings

I feel that there is
nothing more truly artistic
than to love people.

Vincent Van Gogh

DON'T COUNT THE DAYS: MAKE THE DAYS COUNT!

ACT AS IF WHAT
YOU DO MAKES A
DIFFERENCE. IT DOES.

William James

This above all: to thine
own self be true.

William Shakespeare

NO MAN IS USELESS WHILE
HE HAS A FRIEND.

Robert Louis Stevenson

In the sweetness of friendship
let there be laughter.
For in the dew of little things
the heart… is refreshed.

Kahlil Gibran

I'M YOUR NUMBER ONE FAN.

LOOK AT EVERYTHING AS
THOUGH YOU WERE SEEING IT
FOR THE FIRST OR LAST TIME.

Betty Smith

You have to be unique and different and shine in your own way.

Lady Gaga

You are perfectly cast in your
life. I can't imagine anyone
but you in the role. Go play.

Lin-Manuel Miranda

**DARE TO LOVE YOURSELF
AS IF YOU WERE
A RAINBOW WITH
GOLD AT BOTH ENDS.**

Aberjhani

You're a star!

If you're interested in finding out more about our books, find us on Facebook at Summersdale Publishers and follow us on Twitter at @Summersdale.

www.summersdale.com